REMEMBERING WORLD WAR I

LIFE ON THE WESTERN FRONT

Nick Hunter

Heinemann
LIBRARY
Chicago, Illinois

To contact Capstone Global Library please phone 800-747-4992, or visit our website www.capstonepub.com

Edited by Andrew Farrow, Laura Hensley, and
    John-Paul Wilkins
Designed by Joanna Malivoire and Clare Webber
Original illustrations © Capstone Global Library Ltd
    2014
Illustrated by HL Studios
Picture research by Ruth Blair
Production by Sophia Argyris
Originated by Capstone Global Library Ltd
Printed in the United States of America in
North Mankato, Minnesota

042014
008175RP

Library of Congress Cataloging-in-Publication Data

Hunter, Nick.
  Life on the Western Front / Nick Hunter.
    pages cm.—(Remembering World War I)
  Includes bibliographical references and index.
  ISBN 978-1-4329-8082-5 (hb)—ISBN 978-1-4329-8087-0 (pb)— ISBN 978-1-4846-0102-0 (ss)
1. World War, 1914-1918—Campaigns—Western Front—Juvenile literature. 2. World War, 1914-1918—Trench warfare—Juvenile literature. I. Title.

  D530.H86 2014
  940.4'144—dc23   2012042719

Acknowledgments

The author and publisher are grateful to the following for permission to reproduce copyright material: © DACS 2012 p. 40 (via AKG Images); AKG Images pp. 16, 20, 21, 26 (ullstein bild), 34 (IAM), 42 (Mark De Fraeye), 4, 14, 18, 23, 24, 25, 27, 32, 33, 35, 36, 37; Getty Images pp. 5, 10, 17, 19 (Popperfoto), 6, 8, 9, 13, 28, 29, 30, 43 (Hulton Archive), 41 (Fotosearch).

Cover photograph of infantrymen sitting in a trench reading and smoking during the early days of trench warfare in World War I reproduced with permission of Getty Images (Keystone).

We would like to thank John Allen Williams for his invaluable help in the preparation of this book.

Every effort has been made to contact copyright holders of any material reproduced in this book. Any omissions will be rectified in subsequent printings if notice is given to the publisher.

CONTENTS

Some words are shown in bold, **like this**. You can find out what they mean by looking in the glossary.

WHY WAS WORLD WAR I DIFFERENT?

In August 1914, the **empires** of Britain, France, and Russia went to war against Germany and **Austria-Hungary**. The war was the first conflict between Europe's great powers in more than 40 years. For the first time, nations such as France and Germany could call on millions of young men who had been trained to fight for their countries.

The weapons they fought with were more powerful than ever before, with quick-firing machine guns and devastating explosive **shells**. Although few people realized it in the first days, this war would be different from any war before it.

Millions of young men went off to fight in 1914. Most people believed the war would be over quickly and they would soon return home.

TOTAL WAR

The Great War, or World War I as it has since become known, was one of the first "total wars," in which the entire populations of the warring nations were used to win the war. Industry and the people at home worked to supply the huge armies with weapons and supplies.

The war was fought across the world, from the expanses of Eastern Europe to the deserts of Arabia. The United States, Canada, India, and other countries from far beyond Europe would be pulled into the fighting. However, many of the key moments and memories of the war were played out on the shell-shattered, mud-caked battlefields and trenches of France and Belgium—the **Western Front**.

Troops wait to advance toward enemy machine guns on the Western Front in 1917.

In Their Own Words

"At first there will be increased slaughter on so terrible a scale as to make it impossible to get troops to push the battle to a decisive end... Everybody will be entrenched in the next war: the spade will be as indispensable to the soldier as his rifle."

Jan Ivan Bloch in The Future of War (1897) was one of few people who predicted the horrors of World War I

HOW DID THE WAR START ON THE WESTERN FRONT?

When the great powers of Europe went to war in the first week of August 1914, ordinary people generally believed that the war would be short and that their side would be victorious. **Mobilizing** the armies was a huge operation with thousands of trains needed to carry the millions of soldiers up to the front line.

GERMANY'S PLAN

Germany knew it would have to fight both France and its ally Russia. Germany's plan was to attack and defeat France in a quick war and then turn all its forces against Russia. To do this, Germany would have to invade **neutral** Belgium. This invasion brought Great Britain into the war, because the country had promised to defend Belgium if it was attacked, and could not permit a rival power to control territory so close across the English Channel.

Britain's great strength was its navy. The British army in 1914 was small when compared to the giant armies of Germany and France on the Western Front. However, British troops were highly trained, and the British could call on resources from across their empire, including Canadians, Australians, and Indians.

In the early days of the war, troops used bicycles to move quickly to and from the front.

In Their Own Words

"Bands playing, flags flying, a terrific sort of overwhelming conviction that Germany now would go into war and win it very quickly."

Private John Figarovsky, 1st U.S. Division

....

"At 2 o'clock in the morning of the 4th of August we marched out of Freiburg with torches—silent, without any music, without any singing, and with no enthusiasm."

Steffan Westmann, who was called up to join the **infantry** when war broke out

Country	Armies and trained reserves in August 1914	Forces mobilized 1914–1918
France	4,017,000	8,410,000
Great Britain and the British Empire	975,000	8,905,000
Russia	5,971,000	12,000,000
Italy	-	5,615,000
United States	-	4,355,000
Others (Belgium and Serbia)	317,000	2,904,000
Total Allies	**11,280,000**	**42,189,000**
Austria-Hungary	3,000,000	7,800,000
Germany	4,500,000	11,000,000
Turkey	-	2,850,000
Bulgaria	-	1,200,000
Total Central Powers	**7,500,000**	**22,850,000**

This table shows the individual and combined forces of the **Allies** and the **Central Powers**.

BATTLES OF 1914

In August 1914, Germany's bold plan, called the Schlieffen Plan, looked like it might work. Belgium's small army fought bravely, but it was overwhelmed by the powerful German force, which captured the Belgian capital Brussels on August 20. The Germans then advanced to meet the main French and British forces.

France was desperate to regain the Alsace-Lorraine region that Germany had seized after the Franco–Prussian War in 1871. The first French attack was aimed at that region, but it soon broke down with massive **casualties** for the French army.

DID YOU KNOW?

In 1914, many soldiers went to war in uniforms that had changed little for a century. For example, some French **cavalry** wore scarlet pants and plumed helmets. By the end of the war, all forces wore **camouflage** colors, such as gray or khaki. This made them more difficult for enemy guns to pick out.

BATTLE OF THE MARNE

By September 1, Germany's highly trained and efficient forces were threatening Paris, with the French and British retreating. However, the farther Germany advanced away from its own railroads, the more difficult it became to supply the armies, especially with food for the horses that pulled all the **artillery** and supply vehicles. At the Marne River, French forces fought a desperate battle to stop the German army from capturing Paris. Victory there would become known as the "miracle of the Marne," and set the stage for the four years of trench warfare that followed.

WHO'S WHO?

Joseph Joffre (1851–1931)

Joseph Joffre was commander of French forces on the Western Front in 1914. He believed in attacking at all costs, but the French attack into Alsace-Lorraine was a disaster. Joffre was hailed for masterminding the victory at the Battle of the Marne. He was removed from direct command in 1916 as casualties continued to mount on the Western Front.

THE RACE TO THE SEA

The Battle of the Marne saved Paris and France from defeat in 1914. The German forces were forced back to the Aisne River. With their soldiers exhausted and unable to get the supplies they needed, they turned to a defensive tool—the shovel.

The best way for troops to defend themselves against gunfire and artillery was to dig trenches. As both sides dug trenches, their opponents tried to mount attacks around the edge of these new defenses. Some of the fiercest fighting was between German and British forces around the Belgian town of Ypres. Gradually, the line of trenches stretched out until it reached 475 miles (760 kilometers) from the North Sea coast to the borders of neutral Switzerland.

Soldiers digging trenches on the Western Front. For most of the war, both sides were unable to break through the enemy's trench systems.

In Their Own Words

"...of the 1,100 officers and men that came out at the start we have Major Yeadon and about 80 men left. I believe you have plenty of soldiers at home. Well, we could do with a few here."

Corporal George Matheson of the Queen's Own Cameron Highlanders writes home after the First Battle of Ypres

The line of the Western Front moved little from the end of 1914 until spring 1918.

WHAT WAS TRENCH WARFARE LIKE?

From 1914 until spring 1918, both sides made many attempts to break through the enemy's trenches. Hundreds of thousands of men were killed and injured in these battles, but the line of trenches never moved more than a few miles.

The best way to attack a trench was to go around it and attack the enemy along the length of the trench. With trenches stretching from Switzerland to the sea, there were no gaps for this to be possible. This meant that troops could only attack directly toward the enemy trenches.

In Their Own Words

"We were not so much frightened of being killed and wounded as we were depressed by the conditions, as we had thought we were going to fight a glorious war."

Private George Hancox of the Canadian army on his experience of trench warfare

DID YOU KNOW?

At Christmas 1914, British and German soldiers had a brief **truce**. They sang carols and exchanged gifts in the **No Man's Land** between the trenches as they went to bury dead soldiers who lay there. After 1914, commanders ordered that mixing with the enemy should never happen again.

OVER THE TOP

An attack would begin with a huge artillery **bombardment** to destroy the trenches and defenses, such as barbed wire. This often failed and the attackers had to go over the top, leaving their own trenches and advancing through thick mud and craters created by the shells. As the attackers moved forward and struggled to cut through the barbed wire, they were cut down by machine-gun fire. Machine guns could fire hundreds of bullets every minute. If soldiers did manage to capture a trench, the enemy could simply retreat to the next line of trenches. In these attacks, the advancing troops suffered one-third more casualties than the defenders.

TRENCH SYSTEMS

Trenches were not new. They had been used in previous wars, notably the American Civil War of the 1860s. But the trench systems of World War I were bigger and more complex than any that had been used before. German trenches were usually the most complex, while French trenches were often just simple ditches.

DID YOU KNOW?

New trenches were dug with each attack and retreat on the front. Trench systems became confusing, ending in dead ends or shell craters. Signposts and name boards such as "Death Valley" were added to help soldiers find their way around.

At the front of each trench, a raised parapet (bank) made of earth and sandbags faced the enemy across No Man's Land, which could be as little as 80 feet (25 meters) wide. The trenches were not straight, but zig-zagged. This meant that an enemy who got into the trench could not fire along the whole trench and shell blasts would only affect a small area. Trenches were often lined with wood to stop the walls from collapsing.

BUILT TO LAST

Trench systems could include many lines of trenches, linked by winding **communication trenches**, so troops could move around without being seen by the enemy. Trenches included underground shelters, called dugouts, that protected troops from artillery fire. German dugouts were often dug deep into the sides of hills, making them very difficult to destroy.

If their front-line positions were captured, troops could fall back to the next line of trenches.

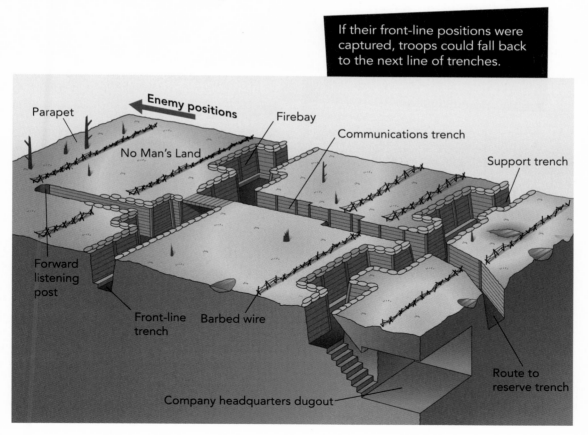

Parapet

Enemy positions

Firebay

No Man's Land

Communications trench

Support trench

Forward listening post

Front-line trench

Barbed wire

Route to reserve trench

Company headquarters dugout

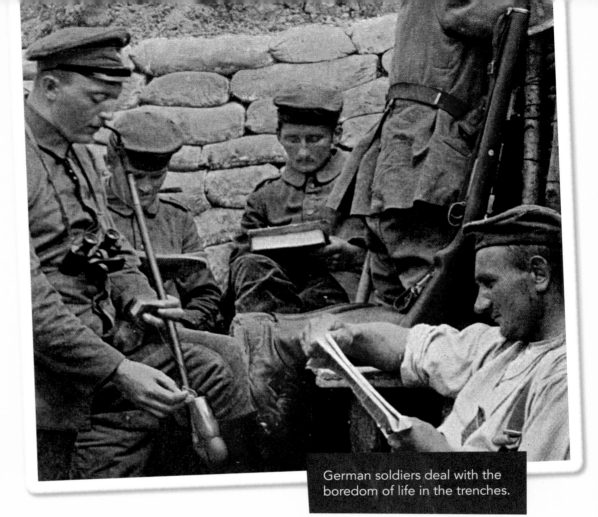

German soldiers deal with the boredom of life in the trenches.

LIFE IN THE TRENCHES

Soldiers always had to be alert for an attack. Anyone sticking their head above the parapet could be picked off by a sniper. The most dangerous times were at dawn and dusk, when attacks were usually launched. At night, troops would repair their trenches and send raiding parties to the enemy trenches.

Soldiers would normally spend a few days at a time in the trenches. While some were stationed in the front line trenches to guard against attack, others would spend their time trying to fight off boredom, cold, and hunger. The noise of the guns and the need to be constantly on alert made sleeping a rare luxury.

DIRTY AND HUNGRY

Conditions could be incredibly dirty. In wet weather, trenches would fill with mud, water, and worse. Common problems included lice that infested everything. Days in wet boots and deep mud caused painful foot **infections**, called trench foot. Food supplies were not always regular and soldiers grew tired of the same food all the time, such as British cans of corned beef called "bully beef."

Sometimes soldiers had to add weeds and plants to soups and stews as their rations were reduced during the war.

In Their Own Words

"Then there were the rats. You would not kill rats because you had no means of getting rid of them, they would putrefy [rot] and it would be worse than if you left them alive. I think they lived in corpses [dead bodies] because they were huge, they were as big as cats."

Fusilier Victor Packer of the Royal Irish Fusiliers

TREATING THE WOUNDED

Millions of soldiers were injured in the brutal trench warfare on the Western Front. Wounded soldiers received first aid in the trenches. They were then transferred to casualty clearing stations where their wounds could be properly treated. Seriously injured soldiers were transferred to hospitals closer to home.

Field hospitals were opened in abandoned factories or other large buildings. As the war went on, and there were more casualties, these field hospitals got bigger, so there was less need to send soldiers home. By 1918, thousands of women nurses were working in these hospitals, including many from the United States, which entered the war in 1917 (see page 37).

As well as injuries caused by the fighting, diseases caused by the conditions in trenches took many men away from the front line. Almost 8 out of 10 British soldiers who were sent home with disease or injury later returned to the war.

Many simple medicines that we take for granted today were not available to medical staff in World War I.

DID YOU KNOW?

One-third of wounded soldiers in World War I died from their injuries. One reason for this was infection. **Antibiotics** to deal with infections were not discovered until the 1920s.

SHELL SHOCK

Thousands of soldiers were affected by the incredible strain of fighting in the war. This led to an illness called **shell shock**, which caused extreme anxiety and mental collapse. The effects of shell shock were not well understood, and many soldiers were accused of being cowards because they could not face fighting. Some were even shot by their own army.

In Their Own Words

"...all the cases were shell-shocked, which meant they couldn't keep their hands or their heads still. I had to hold them gently behind their heads and feed them, and I also used to write their love letters."

Memories of a nurse who treated shell-shocked soldiers

Wounded soldiers lie on stretchers as they wait to be evacuated by train.

Cavalry featured in some of the early battles of the war, but generals soon realized that they were useless against the machine guns and fortified trenches of the Western Front.

HORSES AT WAR

It was not just the soldiers who suffered in the war. Hundreds of thousands of horses also went off to the front. Germany alone mobilized 715,000 horses in 1914. Armies had very few motor vehicles at the start of the war, and these vehicles could not handle the muddy and rough ground as well as horses.

In 1914, most horses were expected to carry cavalry soldiers into battle, but cavalry charges proved no match for the new weapons of war. Instead, horses were put to work pulling the heavy artillery guns into position. Pulling these guns across the blasted landscape was back-breaking work. Horses also carried supplies and pulled ambulances.

"The position over rations for both men and horses was rather precarious... We had strong feelings towards our horses. We went into the fields and beat the corn and oats out of the ears and brought them back [to feed the horses], but that didn't save them."

Gunner J.W. Palmer describes the plight of horses during a retreat in 1914

HORSE INJURIES AND TREATMENT

Horses suffered terribly in the fighting from bullet wounds, shell explosions, exhaustion, and even gas attacks. They also suffered from lack of food and water. The British army Veterinary Corps treated more than 2.5 million horses in France during the war. Around 500,000 of these horses died. Even those that survived were usually sold close to the front when the war ended, rather than being taken back to their previous homes.

Horses were expected to carry heavy loads through the muddy and blasted land of the Western Front.

WHAT HAPPENED AT VERDUN AND THE SOMME?

The United States declared war against Germany on April 6, 1917. The country had tried not to favor either side. Many German-Americans supported the Central Powers, and others did not want to get involved in a European war.

Germany feared American industry as much as American soldiers. This was one reason why they launched unrestricted submarine warfare in January 1917. Any ships supplying the Allies could be sunk without warning. This would probably have been enough to bring the United States into the war, but the final straw was a message from the German government urging Mexico to join the war and attack the United States.

WHO'S WHO?

Erich von Falkenhayn (1861–1922)

Erich von Falkenhayn took charge of Germany's forces in the early months of the war. At Verdun he wanted to make France "bleed to death" so its people would rebel against the war. After huge German losses in the battle, he was removed from command and sent away from the Western Front.

VERDUN

On February 21, Germany launched a massive attack on the important fortress city of Verdun (see map on page 11). They knew that France would use everything it had to defend Verdun. A German victory there could destroy the French morale.

In the first days of the battle, German forces seized a key fort at Verdun. The French brought in waves of **reinforcements** to stop the German advance. When the battle ended in December 1916, the front line was back to the same position as February. France had suffered 400,000 casualties and Germany almost as many.

Collection "Patrie"   GEORGES THOMAS

20 c.
Le récit complet illustré

LA VOIE SACRÉE

The road to Verdun was packed with men, weapons, and ammunition going to the battle, and the dead and wounded being brought back. It became known as the "Voie Sacrée" or Sacred Way.

In Their Own Words

"The commanding officer and all company commanders have been killed. My battalion is reduced to approximately 180 men [from 600]. What am I to do?"

A French Lieutenant signals to his commanders two days after the start of the Battle of Verdun

THE SOMME

France urged the British generals to start their planned attack of 1916 to divert the Germans from Verdun. On June 24, British artillery began a massive bombardment of German forces close to the Somme River. The plan was to destroy the German defenses before a mass infantry attack using many newly trained soldiers.

WHO'S WHO?

Douglas Haig (1861–1928)

British commander Douglas Haig planned two of the war's biggest battles at the Somme and Passchendaele (1917). After the war, Haig was praised for his part in the Allied victory. However, his reputation has declined as people question the **tactics** that cost so many young lives.

Douglas Haig meets with British Secretary of War David Lloyd George during the Battle of the Somme.

"All my best chaps had gone. We buried eight young officers in one grave before we left. It was a terrible massacre. I think the attack should have been called off until the [barbed] wire had been cut."

Captain Alfred Irwin of the British army remembers the first days of the Somme

When British troops went over the top on July 1, they expected little resistance. But the German lines remained intact. Advancing toward the German guns, the British army suffered 57,000 casualties on the bloodiest day in its history. Fighting on the Somme continued until it was ended by heavy rain and snow in November, costing hundreds of thousands of lives on both sides. The Allies had captured some territory, but failed to break the German lines.

Allied soldiers attempt to recover the wounded under heavy German shell fire in the Battle of the Somme.

WHAT WEAPONS WERE USED ON THE WESTERN FRONT?

The weapons of World War I were one of the main reasons for the deadlock of trench warfare on the Western Front. Trenches were dug to protect soldiers from powerful artillery and machine guns. Until the later years of the war, armies did not have the equipment and tactics to combat these weapons and move the front forward.

ARTILLERY

Artillery changed during the war. In 1914, armies relied on field guns that could be moved by horses. Later in the war, these were replaced by bigger guns and cannons called howitzers that were much less mobile, but powerful enough to destroy trench systems. Special vehicles called tractors were used to pull the guns because they were too heavy for horses. The biggest guns of all were mounted on railroad cars and, for some battles, special railroads were built to move these guns.

Huge howitzers pound the German trenches during the Battle of the Somme.

Flamethrowers shot a jet of burning oil over many feet. They were almost as dangerous for the soldier carrying them as for the enemy.

TRENCH WEAPONS

Machine guns had been invented in the late 1800s. Cavalry and infantry armed with rifles were helpless in the face of these powerful weapons. Many soldiers were killed before their commanders found ways of dealing with this threat.

Infantrymen were normally equipped with rifles and razor-sharp bayonets for charging the opposing trenches. As trench warfare continued, other close-range weapons were used. Mortars could fire small shells over a short distance and hand grenades were thrown into trenches if attackers got close enough. Even flamethrowers were used, but these could only be effective over short distances. Wire cutters to get through the coils of barbed wire were an essential part of every army's kit.

NEW WEAPONS

Some weapons were completely new to warfare. These weapons were made possible by advances in technology.

GAS ATTACK

Possibly the most horrifying new weapon was poison gas. Gas was first used by Germany against French soldiers at Ypres in 1915. In this first attack, gas was released from canisters so it would float toward the enemy, but this could be disastrous if the wind changed direction and the gas blew back toward the attackers. In later attacks, gas shells were fired into enemy trenches.

These machine gunners are wearing masks in case of a gas attack.

Both sides used gas during the war, and more than 90,000 soldiers died from the effects of breathing it in. Many more suffered blindness or skin blisters, depending on the type of gas used. By 1918, gas mask technology had improved to protect those under attack.

AIR POWER

Aircraft were another weapon that was new to World War I. At first, their role was spying on enemy positions and checking on the accuracy of artillery fire. By the end of the war, aircraft were bombing enemy trenches and fighter pilots were battling for control of the air.

A photograph taken from an aircraft shows the trench lines, as well as holes and craters caused by explosions.

In Their Own Words

"The horrible part of it is the slow lingering death of those who are gassed. I saw some hundred poor fellows laid out in the sun... drowning from the fluid in their lungs..."

British General Charteris, written in his diary after the first gas attacks in April 1915

DID YOU KNOW?

Flying aircraft on the Western Front was not a safer option than fighting in the trenches. Half of all pilots were killed or seriously injured in action, mostly because of mechanical failure or accidents rather than enemy fire.

As tank technology improved, they were able to deal with the difficult and bumpy terrain on the Western Front.

TANKS

One weapon that would change warfare forever was first seen on the Western Front in September 1916, during the later stages of the Battle of the Somme. The "tank" was originally a code name used to keep them a secret from the enemy, but the name was kept for this armored vehicle.

The enemy was terrified when they saw the tanks, armed with cannons or machine guns, lumbering toward them. The tanks quickly advanced more than 2 miles (3 kilometers) before almost all of them broke down or were stopped by artillery fire.

Early tanks were slow, unreliable, and had no radio contact with each other, but they showed armies a way to escape the stalemate of the Western Front. Tanks would become much more important in later conflicts.

SIGNS OF PROGRESS

In November 1917, tanks proved their worth with a victory in the Battle of Cambrai. More than 400 tanks succeeded in breaking the **Hindenburg Line** for the first time in the war. In a matter of hours, the British advanced almost four miles—farther than they had managed in months of fighting beforehand. Unfortunately, the British failed to exploit their position and much of the ground was lost in a German counter-attack.

France had the most success with the Renault light tank. These tanks were faster than the British versions and were used by U.S. troops in 1918. The Germans built few tanks, preferring to concentrate their efforts on anti-tank weapons to combat the enemy. However, they often used British tanks when they captured them.

HOW DID THINGS CHANGE AFTER THE BATTLES OF 1916?

The battles of 1916 had a big impact on people's opinions about the war. The long lists of casualties from Verdun and the Somme affected communities across Britain, France, Germany, and the wider world. France had been particularly badly hit, and the generals knew that the country could not survive more losses like those of 1916.

The failure of their attack on Chemin des Dames forced many French soldiers to lose faith in their leaders.

MUTINY AND DESERTION

In April 1917, French troops launched an attack at the Chemin des Dames. Once again, they failed to break through the German lines and suffered heavy losses. In the weeks that followed, a wave of unrest swept the French army. Soldiers refused to return to the front line, demanding more food and rest. The "**mutinies**" affected half the French army and meant that much of the Allied fighting during the rest of 1917 was done by troops from Britain and the British Empire. There was also some unrest in the British army as the war dragged on.

Disobeying orders had serious consequences. There were 449 French soldiers condemned to death after the mutinies of 1917, and 27 were actually shot. In the British army, 3,080 soldiers were sentenced to be shot for desertion during the war, although most of these sentences were not carried out.

The largest crater caused by the mine explosions at Messines Ridge was 87 yards wide and 13 yards deep.

DID YOU KNOW?

Mining beneath enemy trenches had been used as a tactic since 1914. The most successful mining operation was in June 1917, when British and Australian forces set off a huge explosion beneath German trenches on Messines Ridge in Belgium. Thousands of German soldiers were killed, and the explosion was heard in London, 130 miles (210 kilometers) away.

PASSCHENDAELE

Generals began to realize that their troops could not take much more of the struggle on the Western Front. But there was little sign that anything had changed in the bloodiest and muddiest battle of 1917.

Stretcher bearers struggle through the deep mud around Passchendaele.

The Battle of Passchendaele was the third battle of the war to be fought around the important area of Ypres, Belgium. The battle is remembered as one of the most wasteful of the war, as 300,000 lives were lost trying to capture land around the village of Passchendaele between July and November 1917. Heavy rain turned most of the battlefield into a sea of liquid mud, and one in four of the British soldiers killed in the battle actually drowned in the mud.

A NEED FOR CHANGE

After the mutinies in the French army during 1917, British forces, including those from **colonies** and **dominions**, took on more of the fighting on the Western Front. Britain had introduced **conscription** in 1916, so almost all men between the ages of 18 and 41 could be called up to the army. The armies could not afford to lose men at the rate they had at the Somme and Passchendaele. Russia was in the midst of revolution and would soon leave the war, so Germany could concentrate more forces on the Western Front. Something would have to change if the Allies were going to win the war.

In Their Own Words

"It was mud, mud, everywhere: mud in the trenches, mud in front of the trenches, mud behind the trenches... I suppose there's a limit to everything, but the mud at Passchendaele—to see men sinking into the slime, dying in the slime—I think it absolutely finished me off."

Bombardier J.W. Palmer of the British army

The soldiers in the trenches were supported by their air forces. Royal Air Force Sopwith Camels, like this one, would have fought German fighter planes over Passchendaele and other battlefields.

35

HOW DID THE ALLIES WIN ON THE WESTERN FRONT?

By 1918, time was running out for all the armies. They were running out of men after the terrible battles of 1916 and 1917. They were also running out of supplies because of naval **blockades**. Politicians and people were running out of patience with the lack of progress on the Western Front.

General Pershing rewards the bravery of some of his troops with medals.

WHO'S WHO?

John Pershing (1860–1948)

General John Pershing had experience of wars in Cuba, the Philippines, and Mexico before he arrived in Europe as leader of the U.S. Army. Pershing was determined to make sure that his army fought under his command, and were not split up to provide reinforcements for the British and French forces.

THE AMERICAN EXPEDITIONARY FORCE

The biggest change in 1918 was the arrival of U.S. troops on the Allied side of the Western Front. The United States had declared war on Germany in April 1917. It took many months to train recruits for the small and inexperienced U.S. Army and transport them by ship. By May 1918, there were 500,000 U.S. troops on the Western Front. By the end of the war, this number had risen to 2 million.

The arrival of U.S. forces raised people's morale in Britain and France. It also convinced Germany that it needed to win the war quickly before the U.S. troops were ready for action.

American artillery shells German forces during their victory at St. Mihiel, France, in September 1918.

In Their Own Words

"It is sad to see the wounded in the hospital, but not nearly as gruesome as on the field where both dead and wounded are strewn about covered with blood. I am just beginning to realize what war really is."

American officer John Clark records his experience of fighting on the Western Front in July 1918

THE END OF TRENCH WARFARE

In spring 1918, the end of fighting in the East enabled Germany to pour more troops on to the Western Front. On March 21, the most ferocious artillery bombardment of the war was followed up by specially selected attack divisions who broke through British lines. By June, the German advance was approaching Paris.

In Their Own Words

"Our lines are falling back. There are too many fresh English and American regiments over there. There's too much corned beef and white, wheat bread. Too many new guns. Too many aeroplanes."

Erich Maria Remarque sums up the German situation in fall 1918 in his novel All Quiet on the Western Front (1929)

At that point the Allies fought back, using tanks, well-aimed artillery, and aircraft as well as infantry. These tactics, used against exhausted armies, had shown the way to win the war on the Western Front and end the deadlock of trench warfare. Allied advances continued, boosted by fresh U.S. forces arriving every month. Germany asked for an **armistice** to end the war in early November, to prevent being invaded by the Allies.

The fast-moving attacks of 1918 were very different from the years of deadlock that had gone before.

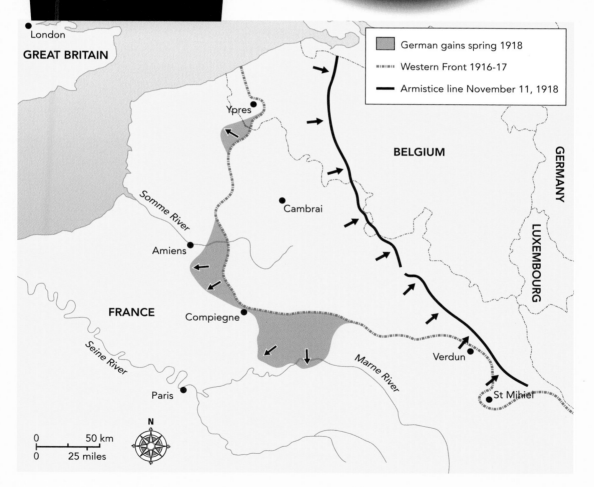

German gains spring 1918

Western Front 1916-17

Armistice line November 11, 1918

GREAT BRITAIN

London

Ypres

BELGIUM

GERMANY

LUXEMBOURG

Somme River

Cambrai

Amiens

FRANCE

Compiegne

Verdun

Seine River

Marne River

St Mihiel

Paris

N

| 0 | | 50 km |
| 0 | 25 miles | |

REMEMBERING THE WESTERN FRONT

We can learn what it was like to fight on the Western Front from the painting, poems, and memories of those who fought in the war. Some of those who fought returned from the war with very visible wounds; others never recovered from the mental stress of the Western Front.

IMAGES AND WORDS OF WAR

Many artists were officially employed to record images of the war, but the scenes they produced were often shocking. After Passchendaele, British artists were banned from showing dead bodies in their pictures.

Otto Dix's Schützengraben, which means "Trenches" in English, paints a grim picture of life in the trenches.

"When you go to war as a boy you have a great illusion of immortality. Other people get killed; not you... Then when you are badly wounded the first time you lose that illusion and you know it can happen to you."

Ernest Hemingway, who was wounded in 1918 while serving in Italy as an ambulance driver

Life in the trenches gave poets and writers plenty of time to write about the war. British war poets included Siegfried Sassoon, Wilfred Owen, and Isaac Rosenberg. German Erich Maria Remarque's *All Quiet on the Western Front* talks about understanding between soldiers on both sides. Not all war writers opposed the war, but they all explored the terrible reality of modern warfare.

WHO'S WHO?

Wilfred Owen (1893–1918)

Owen first served in France at the end of 1916. After heavy fighting in the early months of 1917, he was sent to a hospital in Scotland suffering from shell shock. It was there that he met fellow poet Siegfried Sassoon. Sassoon would become a big supporter of Owen's vivid war poetry, especially after Owen was killed just a week before the armistice.

HONORING THE VICTIMS

In the months that followed the end of the war, countries thought about how they would remember those who had died in the war. Today, the battlefields of the Western Front are home to the graves of the millions who died there. There are more than 400 British war cemeteries in the Somme area alone.

VETERANS DAY

The date November 11, when the fighting ended, is called Veterans Day. It is the day on which the United States remembers those who have died in war. Although this tradition began after World War I, there have been many wars since, and young men and women continue to be killed in conflicts around the world.

It is now difficult to understand why the nations of the world went to war. But we can appreciate the heroism and bravery of those who died in the trenches, and the grief of those they left behind.

The Unknown Soldiers

The injuries suffered by many dead soldiers were so severe that their bodies could not be identified. They were buried in plain graves. In 1921, the bodies of three of these unknown soldiers were buried in Arlington National Cemetery, Virginia, in Westminster Abbey, London, UK, and beneath the Arc de Triomphe in Paris, France. Arlington National Cemetery is the final resting place for more than 400,000 active duty service members, veterans, and their families. More than 3 million people visit the Arlington cemetery each year.

Mourners pay their respects at the Tomb of the Unknown Soldier in Westminster Abbey, London, in 1920.

TIMELINE

1914

July 28–August 4   War is declared, beginning with Austria-Hungary declaring war on Serbia and resulting in Britain declaring war on Germany.

August 7   British Expeditionary Force lands in France.

August 20   German forces occupy Brussels, capital of Belgium.

September 1–6   First Battle of the Marne pushes German troops back from Paris. Trench warfare begins.

October 19   The First Battle of Ypres begins, which ends on November 22.

November   Trenches are dug across the Western Front.

1915

March 10   British attack at Neuve Chapelle fails, partly because of insufficient artillery shells.

April 22   Poison gas is first used as a weapon during Second Battle of Ypres.

May 23   Italy enters the war on the Allied side.

September 25   Allied troops fail to break German lines as Battle of Loos begins.

1916

February 21   Battle of Verdun begins.

May 25   Universal conscription is introduced in Britain, meaning that women are needed to take over many jobs.

July 1   The Battle of the Somme begins, with 57,000 British troops killed or wounded on the first day.

July 23   Australian troops take the lead in the Battle of Pozières Ridge on the Somme, suffering heavy casualties.

September 15   Tanks are used for the first time during Battle of the Somme.

December 18   Battle of Verdun finally ends.

1917

March 8	"February Revolution" in Russia leads to the end of the reign of Tsar Nicholas II and to a new government in Russia.
April	Signs of mutiny occur in the French army after failure of latest offensive.
April 6	The United States declares war on Germany.
June 7	British forces detonate a massive mine explosion beneath Messines Ridge, killing 10,000 German soldiers in seconds.
July 31	Battle of Passchendaele, also known as Third Battle of Ypres, begins.
November 7	"October Revolution" begins in Russia, granting power to the Bolsheviks.
November 20	First large-scale use of tanks brings success at Battle of Cambrai.

1918

March 3	Russia agrees to peace with Germany at Treaty of Brest-Litovsk, releasing German forces to fight on the Western Front.
March 21	German spring offensive begins, pushing Allied forces into retreat.
March 28	American Expeditionary Force plays vital role in battle along the Scarpe River.
July 15	Second Battle of the Marne ends the German spring offensive.
November 11	Armistice is agreed to end the fighting at 11:00 a.m. on the 11th day of the 11th month.

After the war

June 28, 1919	Treaty of Versailles is signed, officially ending the war.
March 4, 1921	U.S. Congress approves the burial of an unidentified soldier in the Tomb of the Unknown Soldier in Washington, DC.

GLOSSARY

Allies countries fighting together against the Central Powers, including the empires of France, Russia, and Great Britain, and later the United States

antibiotics medicines that attack bacteria, which cause infection

armistice agreement to stop fighting

artillery heavy guns and cannons, usually moved around on wheels

Austria-Hungary former European monarchy made up of Austria, Hungary, and parts of other countries

blockade use of warships and other means to prevent supplies from reaching a country. Both sides in World War I tried to prevent food from reaching the other.

bombardment attack using artillery shells and bombs, often coming before an infantry attack

camouflage designed to blend in with the surroundings

casualty soldier killed or wounded in battle

cavalry soldiers on horseback

Central Powers countries fighting against the Allies in World War I, including Germany, Austria-Hungary, and Turkey

colony land that is ruled by people from another country

communication trench narrow trench enabling soldiers and supplies to move between two lines of trenches

conscription forcing all people in a group, such as all men of a certain age, to serve in the armed forces

dominion self-governing country within the British Empire

empire collection of colonies or provinces ruled from another country, such as the British Empire that covered large parts of the world in 1914

Hindenburg Line heavily fortified line of defense built by the German army on the Western Front in 1916–1917

infantry soldiers on foot

infection when tiny micro-organisms, such as bacteria, enter the body through a wound, for example, and cause further illness

mobilize get soldiers or armies prepared and moved into position for war

mutiny rebellion against officers in an army or on board a ship

neutral not supporting or fighting for either side in a conflict

No Man's Land area of land between two opposing trenches, across which fighting takes place

reinforcements additional forces arriving to assist in a battle

shell explosive fired from large artillery or cannons

shell shock mental illness caused by exposure to shell explosions or stress of fighting a war

tactics plans or methods used in trying to achieve something, especially in wartime

truce agreement to stop fighting, often for only a short time

Western Front border of the territory held by the Central Powers and by the Allies in the West, where much of the fighting took place during World War I

FIND OUT MORE

BOOKS

Barber, Nicola. *Living Through World War I*. Chicago: Heinemann, 2012.

Price, Sean Stewart. *Yanks in World War I: Americans in the Trenches*. Chicago: Raintree, 2009.

Ross, Stewart. *World War I (Research It!)*. Chicago: Heinemann, 2010.

Yomtov, Nel. *True Stories of World War I*. Mankato, Minn.: Capstone, 2013.

WEB SITES

www.bbc.co.uk/history/interactive/animations/western_front/index_embed.shtml
This animated map shows how the Western Front changed during the war.

www.kidsworldwar.com/?p=199
Visit this website for a photo gallery showing what life was like in the trenches in World War I.

PLACES TO VISIT

National World War I Museum at Liberty Memorial, Kansas City, Missouri
www.theworldwar.org
Visit the museum to see permanent collections and exhibitions telling the story of World War I.

There are war memorials in thousands of towns and villages around the world. Visit your local memorial and look at the names of the young people who died in the war. You can also visit the Tomb of the Unknown Soldier at Arlington National Cemetery in Washington, DC.

TOPICS FOR FURTHER RESEARCH

- Compare the fighting on the Western Front to conflicts that are happening around the world now. What has changed since 1914?
- You can explore the impact of World War I on your own local area by researching the history of local regiments or soldiers who fought in the war.
- The wearing of poppies in many countries on Veterans Day originated in World War I. What can you find out about the history of this tradition?

INDEX